WEATHER SIGNS

WEATHER REPORT

Ted O'Hare

Rourke

Publishing LLC
Vero Beach, Florida 32964

www.rourkepublishing.com

PHOTO CREDITS: All photos © Lynn M. Stone

Title page: *A rainbow colors the sky at Glacier National Park in Montana.*

Series Editor: Henry Rasof

Cover and interior design by Nicola Stratford

Library of Congress Cataloging-in-Publication Data

O'Hare, Ted, 1961-
   Weather signs / Ted O'Hare
      p. cm — (Weather report)
Includes bibliographical references and index.
Contents: Weather signs — Groundhog Day — Cloud signs — Rainbows and warnings — Plant signs — Mountain signs — Signs of the seasons — Dewdrops — Another weather sign.
ISBN 1-58952-575-2 (hardcover)
1. Weather—Folklore—Juvenile literature. [1. Weather—Folklore.] 1. Title. II. Series. Weather report.
QC998 .O43 2002
551.63'1—dc21   2002151639

Printed in the USA

CG/CG

Table of Contents

Weather Signs   5

Groundhog Day   6

Cloud Signs   9

Rainbows and Warnings   10

Plant Signs   14

Mountain Signs   16

Signs of the Seasons   19

Dewdrops   20

Another Weather Sign   22

Glossary   23

Index   24

Further Reading/Websites to Visit   24

Weather signs

No one can really be sure what today's weather will be like tomorrow or a week from now. But people use weather "signs" to try to help predict the weather.

Some of the signs may be silly ones. For instance, some people who see cows lying down in a field "know" that rain is on the way. The cows are saving a dry spot for themselves!

These cows in Wisconsin are lying down not because rain is on the way, but because they are tired and need milking!

Groundhog day

Every year on February 2, people look to the groundhog for signs about the weather. In Punxatawney, Pennsylvania, if the groundhog comes out of its burrow and sees its shadow, it goes straight back in. This means that winter will last for six more weeks.

On the other hand, if the groundhog doesn't see its shadow, it remains outside. This means that spring is on its way.

The well-known groundhog will go back into its burrow on February 2 if it sees its shadow on that day.

Cloud signs

Cows and groundhogs are one thing. There are, however, some truly helpful weather signs. Clouds are even more helpful when we want to predict the weather. If the clouds are puffy and white, the weather will be fair. If, however, the clouds begin to pile up on top of each other, **thunderstorms** are close by.

When high, thin **cirrus** clouds appear, chances are that heavy rain clouds will soon follow.

A pile of clouds growing into thunderheads means a storm is near.

Rainbows and warnings

A saying you may have heard goes: "Rainbow at morning, sailors take warning." Another one says: "Rainbow at night, sailors' delight." These signs do have some truth in them.

Rainbows occur when sunlight passes through raindrops. If a sailor sees a rainbow late in the day, this means bad weather has passed. A rainbow in the morning means that a new storm is on the way.

"Rainbow at morning, sailors take warning."

Geese flying through the sky on their seasonal migration

Moss, a sign of a moist climate, covers a tree trunk and its roots in a rain forest in Costa Rica.

Plant signs

Plant life can often be a clue to a place's long-term weather, or **climate**. Most plants can live only in certain weather conditions.

Most cactus plants, for example, live only where the climate is warm and dry. Moss grows only in wet climates. Orange trees need warm weather, but they also need some cool weather. **Frost**, however, can damage the crop.

Orange trees will grow only in certain climates that do not have heavy frosts.

Mountain signs

Climate on mountains changes from the bottom of the mountain to the top. The base of the mountain may have forest on one side and desert on the other. The forest side has wet climate, while the desert side is dry.

Trees at the top of many mountains are short and bent. This is because strong, cold winds have bent the trees and shortened them.

Tiny, knee-high spruce trees (right) are a sign that the top of Mount Washington in New Hampshire has a cold and windy climate.

Signs of the seasons

Seasons have climates. Geese and other birds **migrate** southward each autumn. This flight means the end of summer.

Winter is coming when the coats of certain hares and weasels turn white. The coats let the animals blend in with snow and protect them.

Returning birds and plants begin to surface when winter is ending. The days may still be chilly, but the signs are that spring is on its way.

The coat of a snowshoe hare begins to turn white long before the snow begins.

Dewdrops

What is dew? Dew is made up of drops of **water vapor**. The drops condense onto objects such as grass, plants, and even on the roofs of cars and houses.

Dewdrops form when night skies are clear and there is little or no wind. This means there are no clouds, so there is little chance of rain.

Beads of dew cling to a spider web on a clear September morning.

Another weather sign

There's another old saying. "Before a rain, fishes rise and nimbly catch uncautious flies." But why does this mean anything?

Air that is heavy with moisture usually means rain. The insects pick up some of this moisture on their wings. This means they have to fly lower because their wings are heavy. The flies are closer to the water, making them easier for the fish to catch.

Glossary

cirrus (SEER us) — thin white clouds made up of tiny particles of ice

climate (KLY mit) — the type of weather conditions that any place has over a long period of time

dewdrops (DOO DRAHPZ) — drops of water vapor, formed when nights are clear and cool

frost (FRAHST) — a covering of frozen dew

migrate (MY great) — to move with the seasons, usually from a cold place to a warmer place

rainbows (RAIN BOWZ) — optical illusions created when sunlight passes through rain

thunderstorms (THUN dur STORMZ) — the result of large cumulus clouds containing thunder

water vapor (WAW tur VAY pur) — water in its gaseous state; water that is part of the air

Index

cactus plants   14

cirrus clouds   9

climate   14, 16, 19

clouds   9

dewdrops   20

frost   14

groundhog   6, 9

migrate   19

moisture   22

mountains   16

orange trees   14

rainbows   10

thunderstorms   9

water vapor   20

Further Reading

Berger, Melvin and Gilda. *Can It Rain Cats and Dogs? Questions and Answers About Weather*. New York: Scholastic, 1999.

Krupp, E.C. *Rainbows and You*. New York: HarperCollins, 2000..

Strudwick, Leslie. *The Science of Seasons*. Milwaukee: Gareth Stevens, 2001.

Websites To Visit

www.nws.noaa.gov/om/reachout/kidspage.shtml

www.shoal.net.au/~seabreeze/weather.html

www.geocities.com/Heartland/4603/weather.html

www.wilstar.com/skywatch.htm

About The Author

Ted O'Hare is an author and editor of children's information books. He divides his time between New York City and a home upstate.